# Earth Matters

# THREE CHEERS FOR TREES!

## A Book about Our Carbon Footprint

by Angie Lepetit

**Content Consultant:**
Tom Fitz, PhD
Associate Professor of Geoscience
Northland College
Ashland, Wisconsin

CAPSTONE PRESS
a capstone imprint

Every step you take on a beach leaves behind a footprint. So do wet steps on a dry sidewalk or a trek through a muddy yard. Your footprints change the places that you go. **But what does a carbon footprint do?**

A carbon footprint doesn't look like a foot. In fact, you can't see it at all! But it IS a mark you leave behind. **A carbon footprint measures how much you change Earth by using its fossil fuel energy.**

Coal, oil, and natural gas
are fossil fuels. They are found
deep inside Earth. They have given
us energy for many years.
**But once we use them up, they
will be gone forever.**

When fossil fuels are burned for energy, they give off pollution. The pollution acts like a blanket around Earth. **When the blanket thickens, Earth gets hot.**

A hot, polluted planet isn't good for anyone. That's why we need to make good choices about our energy use. **The smaller our carbon footprints, the healthier we keep Earth.**

It takes energy to make stuff. An easy way to shrink your carbon footprint is to reuse items. Old socks can be made into puppets. Empty jelly jars make great piggy banks. By reusing items, we keep factories from making too much stuff. **It keeps Earth clean too!**

Another way to reuse old items is to give them away. Clothes you've outgrown can be given to someone else. So can bikes and shoes. Can you think of other examples?

If you can't reuse old items, it's time to recycle. Put glass, metal, plastic, and paper into bins. Many places will collect them. **It's that easy!**

A big part of our carbon footprint comes from driving. Cars, buses, and trucks add a lot of pollution to the air. **You can keep Earth cooler and cleaner by walking or riding your bike.**

You can greatly reduce your carbon footprint by eating less meat. Raising, preparing, and shipping animals for food takes lots of energy. It makes tons of gases that heat Earth too. **Choosing vegetarian meals is healthy for Earth and for you!**

Lights off! You can reduce your carbon footprint by using less electricity at home. Remember to turn off lights and TVs when they're not in use. In the summer, ask an adult if you can turn up the thermostat a few degrees. **In the winter, turn it down.**

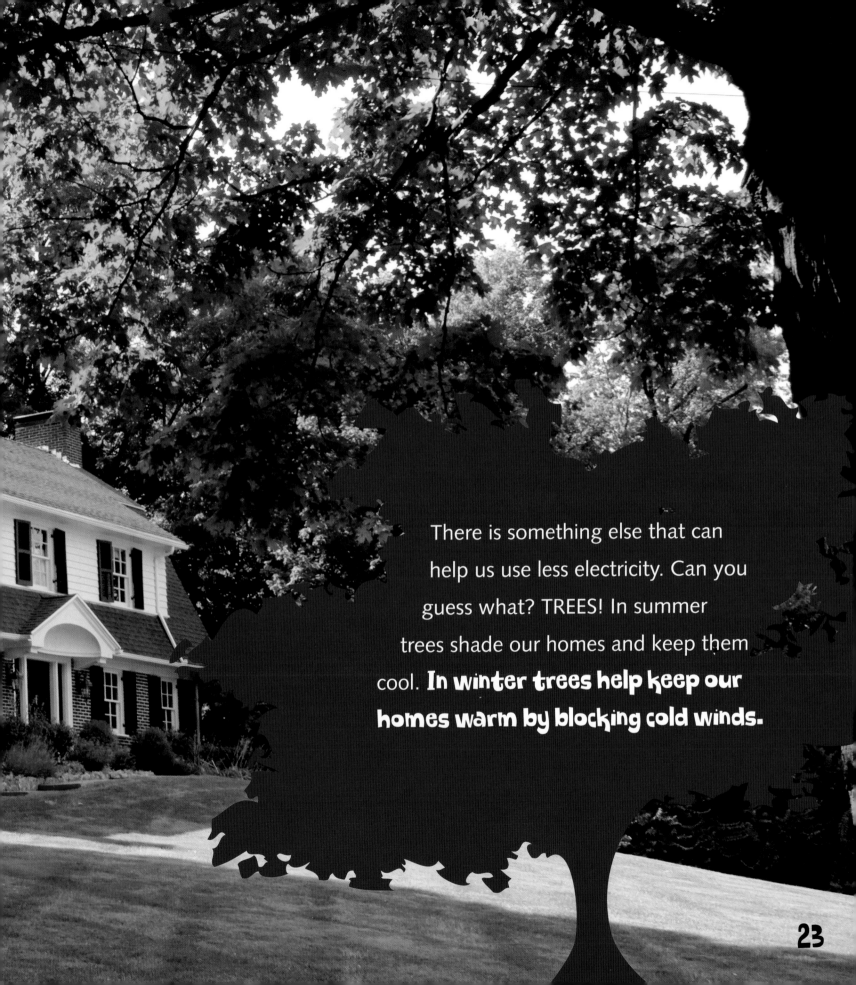

There is something else that can help us use less electricity. Can you guess what? TREES! In summer trees shade our homes and keep them cool. **In winter trees help keep our homes warm by blocking cold winds.**

Trees are also needed to clean the air. They suck up the gas that makes Earth hot. Then trees give us oxygen to breathe. When too much gas is put in the air, trees can't keep up. **This is why we need to use fewer fossil fuels.**

One tree makes enough oxygen for two people to breathe. Let's plant more trees!

25

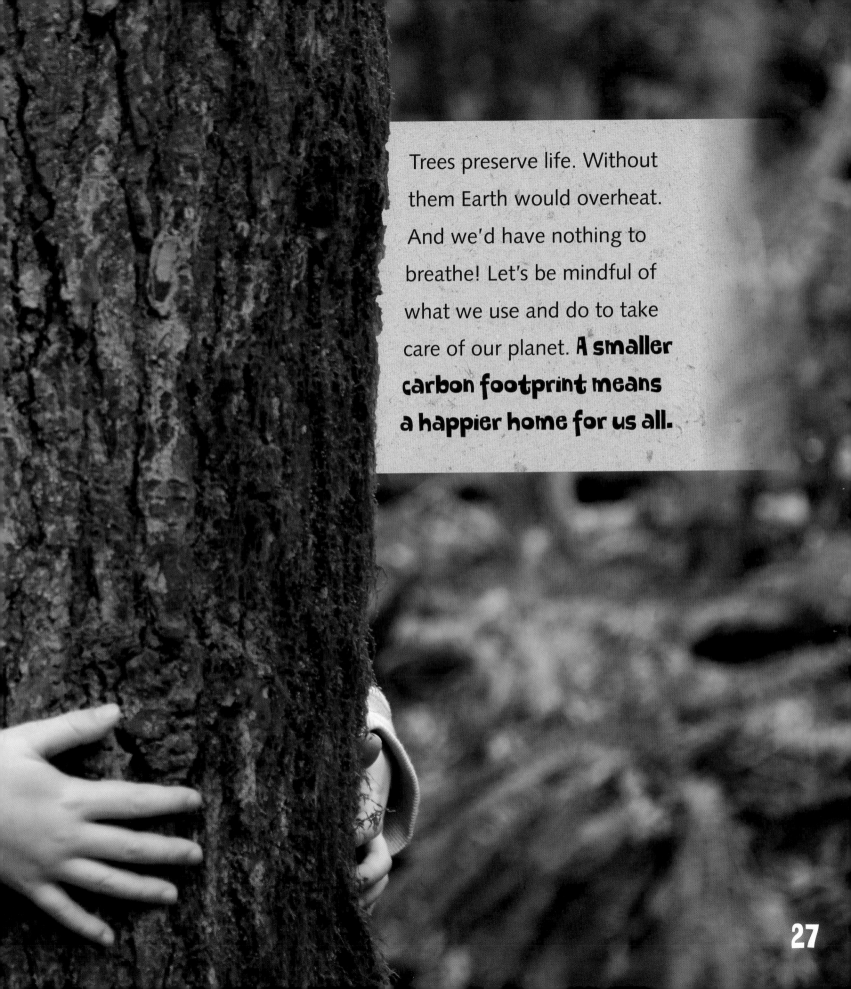

Trees preserve life. Without them Earth would overheat. And we'd have nothing to breathe! Let's be mindful of what we use and do to take care of our planet. **A smaller carbon footprint means a happier home for us all.**

# Make a string-covered vase

Want to reduce your carbon footprint? It's easy to reuse items instead of throwing them away. Here's a fun way to reuse a glass bottle:

## You will need:

Old glass bottle, washed

String or yarn

White craft glue

Toothpick

Scissors

## Instructions:

**1.** Apply glue all around the bottle just below the glass lip.

**2.** Wrap string around the bottle. Use a toothpick to push it down if needed.

**3.** Allow to dry completely.

**4.** Fill it with flowers!

Try using different colors or textures of yarn to create your own unique look.

# Glossary

**degree**—a unit for measuring the temperature of something

**electricity**—a form of energy that can be used to make light and heat or to make machines work

**energy**—the ability to do work

**fossil fuel**—a fuel made from the remains of animals and plants that died millions of years ago

**gas**—a substance that spreads to fill any space that holds it

**invisible**—something you cannot see

**natural gas**—a gas made in the earth that can be burned

**oxygen**—a colorless gas that people breathe; humans and animals need oxygen to live

**pollution**—materials that hurt Earth's water, air, and land

**preserve**—to protect something

**recycle**—to make used items into new products; people can recycle items such as glass, paper, plastic, and aluminum

**reuse**—to use again

**thermostat**—a tool used to measure and control the air temperature

# Read More

**Dickmann, Nancy**. *An Oak Tree's Life*. Watch It Grow. Chicago, Ill.: Heinemann Library, 2010.

**Morrison, Yvonne**. *Earth Matters*. Shockwave Social Studies. New York: Children's Press, 2008.

**Weber, Rebecca**. *Time to Recycle*. Earth and Space Science. Mankato, Minn.: Capstone Press, 2011.

# Internet Sites

FactHound offers a safe, fun way to find Internet sites related to this book. All of the sites on FactHound have been researched by our staff.

Here's all you do:

Visit *www.facthound.com*

Type in this code: 9781620650486

**Super-cool stuff!** Check out projects, games and lots more at **www.capstonekids.com**

# Index

A+ Books are published by Capstone Press,
1710 Roe Crest Drive, North Mankato, Minnesota 56003
www.capstonepub.com

**Library of Congress Cataloging-in-Publication Data**
Cataloging-in-publication information is on file with the Library of Congress.
ISBN: 978-1-62065-048-6 (library binding)
ISBN: 978-1-62065-741-6 (paperback)
ISNB: 978-1-4765-1093-4 (eBook PDF)

**Editorial Credits**
Jeni Wittrock, editor; Bobbie Nuytten, designer; Svetlana Zhurkin, media researcher;
Jennifer Walker, production specialist

**Photo Credits**
Alamy: Myrleen Pearson, cover (left); iStockphotos: Donna Coleman, 12–13; Shutterstock: Alejandro Dans Neergaard, 28 (glue), Alex Staroseltsev, 1 (top), 5, Andre van der Veen, 2–3, Brad Sauter, 6–7, c. (cardboard texture), cover (top), Dmytro Vietrov, 20–21, karnizz, 29 (bottom left), Madlen, 28 (bottle), MJTH, 18–19, Morgan Lane Photography, 14–15, pashabo (recycled paper texture), cover and throughout, Petro Feketa, 29 (right), Rainer Plendl, 26–27, Sergey Zvyagintsev, 28 (scissors), Shebeko, 24–25, spotmatik, 16–17, Stefan Holm, 28 (toothpicks), Steve Mann, 28 (thread), Susan Law Cain, 22–23, Valentina R., cover (right), 1 (right), Vicki France, 8–9, vicspacewalker, 10–11, vovan, 28–29 (back), 30–31, 32

**Note to Parents, Teachers, and Librarians**
This Earth Matters book uses full color photographs and a nonfiction format to introduce the concept of earth science and is designed to be read aloud to a pre-reader or to be read independently by an early reader. Photographs help listeners and early readers understand the text and concepts discussed. The book encourages further learning by including the following sections: Glossary, Read More, Internet Sites, and Index. Early readers may need assistance using these features.

Printed in the United States of America in North Mankato, Minnesota.
092012        006933CGS13